I0485465

How to Make Money Promoting and Selling A Nonfiction Book

By Christine John

http://www.ChristineJohnBooks.com

How to Make Money Promoting and Selling A Nonfiction Book

Copyright © 2015 by Christine John

Email: christinejohnbooks@gmail.com

Website: www.ChristineJohnBooks.com

Front Cover Image: Courtesy of TwoBee at FreeDigitalPhotos.net

Disclaimer:

Although the author has made every effort to ensure that the information in this book was correct at press time, the author does not assume and hereby disclaim any liability to any party for any loss, damage, or disruption caused by errors or omissions, whether such errors or omissions result from negligence, accident, or any other cause.

Table of Contents

Introduction

If you are reading this book right now, you may have reached the point where you have successfully written and published your first, second, or tenth book. Being a self-published author has its advantages in that you are in control of the content and design of your manuscript as well as choosing which online publishing platform you wish to use to publish your book. However, as a self-published author, you also have to be responsible for the marketing and promotion of your own book. This is where many first time, and even established authors get stuck.

Fortunately, this book will show you exactly how you can promote and sell your book to increase book sales. You will learn how to create a sales letter, design a website, set up your author profile, schedule free book promotions, get much needed book reviews, use social media to create more exposure of your book, write press releases, and so much more!

Every author needs to learn how to effectively promote their books to generate sales. By reading this book you will gain the skills needed to successfully market your book to your target audience and boost your book sales. Each chapter explains clearly what you need to do to encourage your readers to buy your book. This book contains step-by-step instructions and clear examples that you can follow easily to achieve your goal.

You can start from the beginning and read the book right through to the end or you can jump to the sections that apply to your needs. At the end of this book you will find a quick action plan or checklist to help you to take each step towards promoting your book and making sales.

Now that you have an overview of what this book is about, it is time to discover all the effective ways you can promote your book to boost your sales. So turn the page and let's get started!

Chapter 1: Create a Sales Letter

Now it is time to write that all important sales letter for your book. This may be the most important task you need to do in order to generate sales. Your sales letter has to grab the reader's attention, peak their interest, explain all the benefits they will gain from reading your book, and show them a fast and easy way to purchase your book.

If you go online and do a Google search, you will find a lot of information on how to write the 'perfect' sales letter, but I am going to keep it simple so that even new writers will be able to create their own sales page. I am going to describe a few basic steps you can take to write a successful sales letter.

What the Sales Letter is Used For

In order for your book to sell you need to write an outstanding sales letter. This letter will help you to get your prospective customers to purchase your book. You can use your sales letter on your website, on the sales page of online book retailers' websites, and in one of your emails to your subscriber list. So here are a few steps you can take to write your very own sales letter.

Identify Your Target Audience

Many authors tend to overlook this step when writing a sales letter. But it is very important to know who your target audience is and how you are going to persuade them to purchase your book. For example, are you writing a weight loss book for men, women, or children? What age group are you targeting? Do you want to market your book to prospective buyers in a particular country or region? These are some of the questions you should ask yourself when considering your target audience and writing a sales letter aimed at them.

Grab the Reader's Attention

The first step in writing a sales letter is to grab the attention of your audience. You can do this by writing a compelling headline. Asking a question at the start of your sales letter is a great way to grab the reader's attention and gives them a reason to continue reading down the page.

Use Low Competition Keywords

Keywords help to drive traffic to your sales page. They are also used by the search engines to find relevant content on your page. You can include keywords in your headline and two or three times in the body of your sales letter. Visit Google Keyword Planner to search for the best keywords with low competition to use on your sales page.

Arouse Interest by Listing the Benefits

This is the part where you answer the question "What's in it for me?" by listing the benefits of your book in bullet points. First make a list of all the problems your potential customer may be facing which she needs to solve. Each problem you answer can be labelled as a benefit.

For example, your book can make them look more attractive, improve their health, make them feel good about themselves, give them more energy, etc.

Build Up the Desire to Purchase Your Book

This next step is to stimulate the desire of your prospective customers and appeal to their emotions so that they will want to buy your book. Your offer should be so irresistible that your audience will place an order for your book immediately. You can include case studies, testimonials, or quotes from experts to help reassure your potential customers that your offer is genuine and the information in your book will help solve their problems.

Include a Clear Call to Action

There are several ways you can prompt your prospective customer to take action and buy your book. You can offer a 100% money back guarantee. You can also add a couple of free bonuses that the reader can get when they buy your book. Additionally, tell your prospective customers exactly what they need to do to purchase your book. Make it as easy as possible for them.

Advantages of writing a sales letter

One of the best ways to boost the sale of your book is to write an attention grabbing sales letter. There are several advantages that you gain when you write a sales letter for your book, which include the following:

1. Sales letter writing increases book sales immediately.
2. A sales letter helps to capture the interest of your target audience.
3. The sales letter provides sheer benefits of your book
4. It shows that your book can solve problems that people find in their day-to-day lives.
5. The sales letter will help you to develop a relationship with your prospective customers so that they trust you and your book.

Bonuses

One thing you can include on your sales page is the offer of two or three bonuses as a way to thank your customers for purchasing your book. This also creates value and makes the customer feel as though you are giving away additional valuable information for free just for buying your book. These bonus items can be other e-books or downloadable products such as videos or software.

There are four things to keep in mind if you decide to include bonus items in addition to your e-book on your sales page:

1. Ensure that your bonuses are relevant to the topic of your e-book. For example, if your e-book is about weight loss you can include a low fat recipe book and calorie counting software as bonuses.

2. The best thing to do is offer three carefully chosen bonus items that will add value to your own e-book instead of adding dozens of irrelevant titles.

3. Instead of trying to write another book to offer as a bonus, you can use PLR e-books and repots which you can get cheaply or free of charge. Before you use any PLR products, make sure that you read the reproduction rights. Some PLR e-books allow you to modify the cover page

and the contents in the book, whereas others may restrict you from making any changes at all to the book.

4. You can include many different types of items as bonuses on your sales page. You can offer a book of case studies, an interview with an expert, a collection of useful websites, or audio files such as podcasts that may come in the form of MP3's that people can download and listen to on their iPad, tablet or mobile phone.

Don't forget to give a description of each of the bonuses you are offering as well. Sometimes people may buy your book simply to get their hands on the free bonuses.

Great Sales Page Examples

To conclude this chapter on sales letter writing, I have provided links to five great sales pages for you to examine. These are sales pages of three top-selling Clickbank products:

Guilt Free Desserts - http://www.guiltfreedesserts.net/
The Three Week Diet - http://www.3weekdiet.com/?hop=0
Ryan Shed Plans - http://www.myshedplans.com/go/

Chapter 2: Set up an Author Page on Amazon's Author Central Website

The Author Page on Amazon's Author Central website is a great way for readers to learn more about you and for you to sell more books. Amazon lists your books on this page so that readers can browse through your books and make purchases. The following instructions show you how to set up your Author Page at the Author Central website.

1. First, go to https://authorcentral.amazon.co.uk and set up your Author Central account.
2. In the Author Central, click the Profile tab. You'll see sections where you can add or change your biography, photos, videos, and events.
3. Click the **add** or **edit** link next to a section. Instructions appear, along with space to add information.

If you need any help with making changes to your Author Page simply visit the Help page on the Author Central website at https://authorcentral.amazon.co.uk/gp/help.

There are some things you can do to make your Author Page grab the attention of your readers. One way is to ensure that all of your books are listed on your page. Click on the Books tab at the top and then click the **Add More Books** button. Enter the title, author name or ISBN number of your book and click the **Search** button. When your book appears click on the **This is My Book** button. It may take up to 5 days for your book to appear in the list.

Click on the Author Page tab. On the right side of the page you can add photos, videos and your Twitter feed as well. In the photo section make sure that you upload a photo of yourself that you also used on your website and on social media. In the video section you can add your video book trailers so that people can get an idea what your book is about from watching the videos. To add your Twitter feed simply click Add Account in the Twitter section.

When you write in the Biography section of your Author Page, make sure that the information you provide is something that helps the reader to know more about you and how your books can help them. Talk about your book. What benefit does your book offer the reader? What makes your book different from other books? Also mention who would want to buy your books. Don't forget to write a short paragraph about yourself and include a call to action by telling the reader to scroll down the page to check out your other books, if you have any other books listed.

Your author bio is the first thing that people see when they visit your Page and this may help you to sell more books. Just make sure that you keep updating your Twitter feed so that people will see that you are active on social media.

Chapter 3: Optimize Your Book for Amazon

Amazon has millions of books listed on its website and you want to make sure that your book will be seen by the millions of visitors the online retailer receives on a daily basis. So how do you make people more aware of your book on Amazon? The following tips can help you to make your book more visible on the Amazon marketplace.

Tip #1: Use keywords to optimize your book listing on Amazon.

Keywords can be used when you write the description of your book after you have uploaded it to the website. If you did keyword research for your book and have a list of the primary search terms covered in the topics of your book then you can include those keywords in your description.

For example, if you wrote a book about camping the keywords you would use are camping, caravanning, family camping trip, camping holiday, campers guide, tents, sleeping bags, lanterns, camping manual, and camping destinations. When a reader uses any of those terms in Amazon's search box, your book will show up in the results.

Tip #2: Set up a Personal Profile on Amazon and post reviews.
Your personal profile is about you as a book buyer, not as an author. Log in to your Amazon account. On the far left you'll see your name's Amazon.com, for example, Christine's Amazon.com. Click there and then click on the blue tab at the top of the page that reads "My Profile".

Use the edit function to upload a photo, add a biography about yourself, your website, and signature. It is important to include your signature because it is a tag line that shows up after your name when you post reviews on Amazon. You can use your signature to advertise your business and website.

When you are satisfied with your personal profile you can start posting reviews of books you've read. When you do this, your name and signature will appear on each review.

Tip #3: Use the Look Inside Your Book feature.
Amazon allows its customers to browse and download a few pages of your Kindle book before purchasing. This feature helps customers to find your book more easily when they search on Amazon and it increases book sales. Usually Amazon

automatically adds this feature to your book listing, but if you find that this feature is not active on your book sales page then you need to enrol your book in the Look Inside program. Go to http://amzn.to/1Y5fOQ7 to find out how to submit your book to the program.

Tip #4: Choose the right category.

When you are in the process of publishing your book, Amazon allows you to list your book in two categories. It is important that you position your book in the right category because this helps book buyers to find your book. It's not always easy to find the best categories for your book. If you are having trouble with this, the best thing to do is look for books that are similar to yours and check what categories they're in. This will help you to find the appropriate category for your book.

For example, go the book's sales page and scroll down to the bottom of the page. You will find the different categories the book is listed in and this will give you an idea of where your book will fit in. If you cannot find these categories you can contact Amazon and ask them to list your book in the appropriate category.

These four tips are free, easy to use and don't take much time to set up. Make sure that you follow these tips so that you will see a boost in your book sales on Amazon.

Chapter 4: Get Book Reviews

I believe that people will be more inclined to buy your book if your book has received a lot of positive reviews. You need book reviews because this will help you to sell more books. Unfortunately, it is very difficult for self-published authors to get reviews. In addition to requesting readers to review your book after they read you should also submit your book to review sites. Here is a list of websites that do book reviews:

The Swanky Bibliophiles
http://achaury.wix.com/bibliophilebookrevs

The Reader Girl http://www.thereadergirl.com/

The Paperback Pursuer
http://thepaperbackpursuer.blogspot.co.uk/

Reading Shy with Aly http://readingshy.blogspot.ca/

You can also check out the following directories which list book reviewers:

The Book Blogger List http://bookbloggerlist.com/

Book Review Directory
https://bookreviewdirectory.wordpress.com/

eBook Crossroads http://www.ebookcrossroads.com/book-reviewers.html

When you make a request to get your book reviewed, be polite and courteous. Also make sure that you read through the book review request guidelines before your submit your book for review. The following is an example of how you can write a request for a book review:

BOOK REVIEW TEMPLATE
(Replace what is in **Bold** and in the [brackets] with your own information.)

Dear **[Name of Reviewer],**

My **[Genre]** book, **[Title of Book]** was released / is to be released on **[Date]** and is **[Word Count]** words in length.

I visited your blog, **[Blog Name],** and enjoyed your **[Blog Post / Review of a Particular Book / Research Note]**. Please consider my book **[Title of Book]** for review.

Blurb: **[Description of Book]**

You can read a sample chapter here: **[Link to Sample Chapter]**, or view more about the book at my author website here: **[Link to Website]**.

If you would like a complimentary review copy **[specify copy the Reviewer prefers mentioned in the review submission guidelines]** please let me know.

Thank you for your consideration.

Sincerely,

[Name]
[Email]
[Website]

Here is an example of an email sent to a fictitious book reviewer to get my book *How to Write a Nonfiction Book that Sells* to be reviewed:

Dear Joe Brown,

My nonfiction book **How to Write a Nonfiction Book that Sells** was released on 30th August 2015 and is 10600 words in length.

I visited your blog, Joe's Book Blog and enjoyed your review of the book **Publishing on Kindle the Write Way** by Dorothy Doe. Please consider my book **How to Write a Nonfiction Book that Sells** for review.

Blurb:

Need help writing a book?

Can't think of a good topic to write about?

Need to find the easiest and fastest way to edit your book?

If you answered 'Yes' to all of these questions, then you need to read **How to Write a Nonfiction Book that Sells** by Christine John. This book provides you with great tips and sound advice to help you overcome your writing obstacles.

Christine John has been writing for over 15 years and has authored and published books on a wide range of topics such as web designing, online business, and job search, as well as short stories, novels and poetry.

In the book **How to Write a Nonfiction Book that Sells** *Christine will share her strategies for writing a nonfiction book that people will want to read.*

How to Write a Nonfiction Book that Sells *is an essential guide that every aspiring author needs to read to help them write a successful nonfiction book.*

You can read a sample chapter here: http://www.christinejohnbooks.com/nonfictionbooksells or view more about the book at my author website here: http://www.christinejohnbooks.com/how-to-write-a-nonfiction-book-that-sells.

If you would like a complimentary review copy in PDF format please let me know.

Thank you for your consideration.

Sincerely,

Christine John
ChristineJohnBooks@gmail.com
http://www.ChristineJohnBooks.com

Chapter 5: Start a Free Book Promotion Through KDP Select Program

To jumpstart your book promotion, if you have published your book using Kindle Direct Publishing, you can enrol your book in the KDP Select Program and schedule a free book promotion. I highly recommend that you schedule a five day free book promotion if you just published a new book so that you can gain more exposure of your book, get as many downloads as you possibly can, and get book reviews of your new book.

Once you have enrolled your book in the KDP Select program you cannot publish your book anywhere else during the enrolment period. The program lasts for three months and during this time you have the opportunity to use five days within the enrolment period to promote your book for free. Follow the instructions below to schedule your free book promotion days.

1. Go to the Amazon website and scroll down to the bottom. Click **"Independently Publish with Us"** and click **Sign In** at the top right side of the page to sign in to your account.

2. As soon as you sign in, you will be directed to the Bookshelf page. This section displays all the books you have published. On the right side of your book, under Book Actions, click **Enrol in KDP Select.**

3. A pop up box will appear asking you to confirm that you want to enrol your book in KDP Select. Click **Enrol**.

4. The same button that you clicked on to enrol your book in KDP Select will then change to **Promote and Advertise**. Click on this button to view the options you have to promote your book.

5. There are two ways you can promote your book on Amazon. You can either sign your book up for a Kindle Countdown Deal or a Free Book Promotion, but you can only choose one for each enrolment period. For now we will focus on promoting your book for free during this enrolment period. Select **Free Book Promotion** and then click on the button **Create a New Free Book Promotion**.

6. You are allowed five days to promote your book for free. Enter the start date and end date of your free book promotion days and then click **Save Changes**.

7. Once it has been saved, scroll down to the bottom of the page and you will see the date your free book promotion starts and ends. You have the option to edit the scheduled

promotion in order the change the dates or you can delete it if you want to cancel the promotion.

8. Once you are satisfied with your scheduled free book promotion, you can either click on the Bookshelf tab at the top of the page to return to the books page or you can sign out.

Chapter 6: Create an Author Website

Every author should have a website in my opinion. As an author having a website can help you to build your online presence, promote your books, and build a subscriber list of fans who love your work. Whenever you publish a new book, you can easily let your fans know by emailing them and this can help you to boost book sales.

Building a website may seem like a very difficult task, but it is quite easy to build and you don't have to worry about knowing any complicated CSS or HTML codes to create one. One of the best website design software to use is WordPress. This software makes it easy for anyone to create a website or blog.

A great way to get started building your website is by following instructions in my book *WordPress for Beginners: The Easy Step-by-Step Guide to Creating a Website with WordPress.* The first thing you need to do before you can create a website is to first register a domain name and set up web hosting.

Register a Domain Name

A domain name is the name of a particular website. An online user would type a domain name in order to gain access to a website on the internet. For example, the domain name of my website Christine John Books is ChristineJohnBooks.com. The domain name appears in the address bar of your web browser.

There are many websites that offer domain registration. The one I use is DomainOrb (www.DomainOrb.com). I pay only $9.99 per annum for registration and I renew it every year.

It's not easy coming up with a unique domain name because it seems like the best ones are already being used, but you can try using a dictionary or thesaurus to come up with a domain name. You can also think of the niche market you are targeting and use that as a domain name. For example, if you have written a book that targets people who have skin problems such as acne, you could create a domain name called GetRidofAcne.com.

Once you have decided on your domain name and have registered it, the next step is to find a web host to host your website.

Set Up Web Hosting

A web host is an online company that stores all the pages of your website and then transmits it on the internet for people to view. There are thousands of companies on the internet that offer web hosting, but the one I use is Just Host (www.JustHost.com). All you have to do is visit their website to sign up, follow the instructions to set up your web hosting account and they will send you an email to confirm that your account has been set up. The email will also include Nameservers which will allow you to link your domain name to your web host.

Build Your Website

Hopefully at this stage you have already purchased your domain name and set up web hosting. Now it's time to start thinking about how you are going to set up your website. You can start off by creating a basic website which should consist of the following pages: Homepage, About, Books, Contact, Events, Blog, and Resources.

Homepage

Your homepage is the first page that people will see when they visit your website. Make sure that you fill it with enough information that tells your visitors what your site is about, but try not to cram too much information on the page. The main items you should have on your homepage are:

- **Your latest book.** Include a cover image of your book and place it in the centre of your homepage. Also include a brief description of the book and a link to purchase the book.

- **Brief Description of Other Content.** Show links to some of your blog posts, to your resources page, or to your books page. This section should give people an idea of what your site has to offer.

- **Headshot and Author Bio.** Include your headshot and a brief bio about yourself that ends with "Read More" which links to your About page. Ensure that you use the same headshot for your social media sites like Facebook, Twitter, LinkedIn, Google+, etc.

- **Email Subscription Form.** You need this to get people to subscribe to your website so that you can email them about any future titles, special promotions, and useful articles, information and products they can use.

- **Social Media.** Add social media buttons that people can click on to connect with you online.

Check out Joanna Penn's website www.TheCreativePenn.com. The homepage on her website is the perfect example of how you should set up your own homepage.

About Page

This is the page where you give a brief description of yourself as an author and what you do. Include a headshot, same as the one you would use on your homepage, and write a short bio about yourself. You can divulge some background information about yourself, but an even better use of this page is to show readers how qualified you are to solve their problems. Use this section to let readers know how they will benefit by reading your books.

Your author bio should consist of information about the core benefit that you offer to your readers and why your books are unique. Let your readers know who would buy your books. This allows you to focus on your target audience. You can mention a few hobbies and any accomplishments that are relevant to the books you write. Keep it short and simple. Additionally, you should always include a Call-to-Action. This is a simple command in which you tell your readers to check out the other books that you have to offer.

Books

On this page make it easy for your readers to find all of the books you have written in one place. On this page you should have images of your book covers, the title of each book, a short description, links to where buyers can purchase your book, and a "Read More" link which leads to a single page for each of your books.

Single Page for Each Book

If you have several books that you have written you need to create a single web page that is dedicated to each of your books. On this page you should include the book cover, title, a full description, any reviews or testimonials about the book, and links to buy the book. You can also include a book trailer video of your book on this page if you have one.

Contact

You should place a contact form that people can fill in to get in contact with you. Make it as easy as possible for visitors to your website to be able to connect with you. Include your email address, mailing address and links to your social media networks such as Facebook, Twitter, etc.

Events

This page is not for every author and it is optional if you want to include it on your website. Use this page to inform your readers of dates of your book tours and what cities you will be visiting. Also include venues where you have spoken before and how you can be contacted to set up an event.

Blog

Make sure that you have a lot of information to post on your blog. You can blog about your book and topics that are relevant to your book. List your name as the author of the post so that your readers may know that it is actually you that is writing. Allow people to be able to leave comments at the end of your posts and also make it easy for them to share your blog posts through social media.

Sidebar

Most websites have a sidebar and this is a great place to get readers to subscribe to your website. All you need to include in your sidebar is an email subscription box, a headshot and short bio, an image and link to your latest book, and popular posts.

Resources

Your resources page is a great way to share your content. On this page you can include other products and services that are relevant to your market niche which can help your readers. Include videos, tips on writing, interviews, and free sample chapters of your books that your readers can download.

These are some of the pages you can include to make your author website. Tim Grahl provides a lot more information about building the ultimate author website. Check out the information he provides on his website at http://timgrahl.com/how-to-build-the-ultimate-author-website-in-1-hour.

Website Statistics

Once you have set up your author website, you can find out the number of visitors to your website and where they come from. You can also check which keywords are driving traffic to your website. You can do this and much more by using a free web tracker tool called StatCounter (https://statcounter.com/) or Google Analytics. I prefer to use StatCounter because it is easy to sign up and you can install the plugin if you are using WordPress.

Chapter 7: Submit to Search Engines

Search engines are websites that allow online users to search for specific information on the World Wide Web using search terms called keywords. Examples of search engines are Google, Yahoo and Bing. These are the three most popular search engines on the internet. If you want to get traffic to your author website then be sure to submit your site to these search engines. You may be required to create a free email account on each of these sites in order to submit your website. Visit the following search engines to get started.

Google https://www.google.com/webmasters/tools/submit-url
Yahoo https://search.yahoo.com/info/submit.html
Bing http://www.bing.com/toolbox/submit-site-url

In addition to submitting your site to the search engines, you can also ping your site's URL. Pinging your author website is a great way to get noticed by all the search engines and online directories so that your site gets indexed quickly. This can also lead to increased traffic to your website. But you should only ping your website if you have added new content.

Most ping tools are free and easy to use. All you have to do is enter your site's URL and hit the Submit button. The ping tool will then add a link to your site to hundreds or even thousands of search portals and other services. The following are ping tools that you can use to drive traffic to your website:

Pingomatic http://pingomatic.com

Ping My Link http://www.pingmylink.com

Pingler https://pingler.com

Chapter 8: Build a List

Every author needs to build an email list of subscribers. It is important to have an email list because this is the most direct way to communicate with your subscribers. You can easily promote your books by sending an email to your list. This is a great way to make money from book sales.

I recommend using Mail Chimp (http://mailchimp.com/) to begin building your email list because it is free to sign up and Mail Chimp offers different packages according to your business needs. If you are just beginning to build your email list then I suggest that you choose the Entrepreneur package. This allows you to send 12,000 emails to 2,000 subscribers for free. No credit card required.

Other popular email service providers are Aweber, Get Response, and Constant Contact. All of these email list building services provide you with all the tools, templates and services you need to get subscribers and manage your email list.

Once you have signed up to one of these providers, the next step is to create a compelling offer that will attract your prospective subscribers. This could be an e-book, a short report, a free webinar, a podcast, a video, or the promise of discounts or deals exclusively for your subscribers.

The next step is to create an opt-in form. Your email service provider will provide you with tools to create an opt-in form for your website. The only information you need to ask for at this stage is simply the subscriber's first name and email address. If you ask for any other information they most likely will not complete the process.

Once you have created your opt-in form, you need to add it to your website. This is as simple as copying and pasting a snippet of code provided by your email service provider. You can place the opt-in form on the right sidebar of your website, at the top of the sidebar, after each blog post, in your site's footer, or on your About page.

Now you need to start getting subscribers. There are several ways you can build your email list. One way is to offer your services in exchange for a few mentions in the internet marketer's newsletter. For example, if you are good at making videos you could offer to create a video to promote the marketer's products in exchange for the marketer to include a link to your website in their newsletter.

Another way is to hold a giveaway. You can give away something that is valuable to your target market such as a digital product in exchange for people's email addresses.

Guest blogging is a very effective way to get subscribers. If you write a guest post on a popular website, this will help you to increase your visibility online and gain new subscribers. Make sure that you write a guest post that is relevant to your niche market.

When you start getting subscribers you need to ensure that they remember who you are and why they signed up to receive emails from you. Therefore, in your first email you should include an introduction telling your subscribers who you are so that they don't forget you, include a photo of yourself, introduce your product without being salesy or pushy, and let your subscribers know what to expect in the series of emails you will be sending them. At the bottom of every email you should also include a reminder of what the subscriber signed up for.

For more information on how to write compelling emails that your subscribers will be happy to read, check out this article on writing emails: http://www.quicksprout.com/2015/06/24/how-to-write-emails-your-subscribers-cant-wait-to-open/

Chapter 9: How to Promote Your Book Using Twitter

Social media is a very powerful tool that authors need to use to promote their books. It is not enough to simply tweet about your book or make an announcement on Facebook that your book has been published. You need to do so much more to grab the attention of book buyers to get them interested in your book. There are several ways you can do this by using Twitter, Facebook, YouTube, and other social media networks. The first one we will look at is Twitter.

Many authors say that Twitter is the best social media site for promoting and selling books. Twitter is more like an instant messaging system which people use to send very short messages, called tweets, which are up to 140 characters in length to a list of followers. Authors use Twitter to post about their books, their writing, and their interests.

Where do You Start?

Sign up to create a Twitter account. Write a short bio about yourself and be sure to include a link to your blog or website. Also include a photo of yourself or your book cover. It's your choice.

Following and Being Followed

With Twitter you can find people in your niche and follow them. In return some of them may follow you. Here is a great way to get Twitter followers:

1. Search for popular authors who have published books related to your niche.
2. Visit their profile and click on the "Followers" link.
3. Go through the follower list and look for people who are following your author.
4. Click on the "follow" button on those you find will most likely be interested in your book.

If you follow these steps for a few minutes every day you will be able to follow at least 20 or 30 people on Twitter. In a few days you will notice that 10 to 15 of those people will follow you back.

Using Twitter

Once you have gained new followers on Twitter, the next step is to post tweets regularly to promote your book. Your tweets need to be interesting and informative. You can't keep saying over and over "Buy my book" on Twitter because people will ignore your messages and many of them will also stop following you. There are only 140 characters you can use to write a message, so you need to think carefully about the kind of message you want to share with your followers. Here are a few tips that you can apply when communicating with others on Twitter.

Know Your Audience.

Find out what kind of people would be interested in reading your book. Do research on the kind of topics they would be interested in. Search for authors who have books similar to yours and look at some of the topics they tweet about. Make sure that you tweet about topics that your target audience finds interesting. For example, if you wrote a book about weight loss, your tweets should be about foods and exercises that help you to lose weight. Your tweets will attract followers who are interested in these topics, and many of them will buy your book.

Post Tweets that People will want to Read

Many authors find it very challenging to come up with an interesting message using only 140 characters. But it can also be an opportunity for writers to be more creative. You can tweet an inspirational message relevant to your book, give an update of the progress you have made in writing your book, tweet links to articles that your followers may find useful, and thank people for giving a positive review about your book.

Use a Link Shortener.

Because Twitter has restricted the number of characters you can use to post tweets, one of the things you will have to do is shorten your URL. Use bit.ly, buff.ly, tinyurl (free to use online), or any other link shortener to fit your URL into your tweet. When you add an Amazon link in your Twitter posts, use BookLinker. This is a free universal Amazon link shortener. When readers click on the link, it opens the book's page of their country's Amazon website, e.g. Amazon.co.uk for United Kingdom and Amazon.com for United States.

Use Hashtags to Emphasize Keywords.

A hashtag is a symbol used to help people who are interested in a particular topic to find you on Twitter. Choose one or two words that will capture the interest of your target audience and simply put a hashtag (#) before the words in your tweet. For example, if you wrote a book about camping you may want to hashtag #camping, #campingdestination, #tents, #lanterns, and #campholidays.

Use Twitter to get Book Reviews.

You can post a tweet offering free copies of your e-book for anyone who wants to write a review on Amazon, on their blog, or on any other bookselling website. Getting book reviews can help boost sales of your book.

Interact with Your Followers

Ask your followers questions about their interests. If they ask you a question, reply immediately. Read some of their tweets and respond to them. If they mentioned that they read your book and enjoyed it, ask them what they liked best about your book. Thank them for reading it. This will encourage the reader to talk about your book, share it with others, and to buy your next book.

The following is a list of book bloggers on Twitter that you should follow:

http://twitter.com/#!/BiblioBrat

http://twitter.com/#!/bookaliciouspam

http://twitter.com/#!/amusedbybooks

http://twiter.com/#!/YABookShelf

http://twitter.com/#!/brokeandbookish

Chapter 10: How to Use Facebook to Promote Your Book

Facebook can be a very powerful tool to include in your book marketing campaign. In addition to setting up a personal profile, you can also create a fan page and use paid advertising services that Facebook offers to broadcast your message to thousands of Facebook users. Additionally, you can boost posts to promote your book to increase book sales. Once you have set up your personal profile, the next thing you need to do is create a Facebook page.

How to Create a Facebook Fan Page

Creating a fan page is the first step in promoting your book on Facebook. You can use your fan page to keep in touch with your readers, build your brand, and be able to respond quickly to your readers' comments, feedback, and questions. Simply follow the steps below to create your fan page.

Step 1: Choose a category and page name.

The name of your fan page helps your fans, readers, and prospects to find you easily. It also lets people discover instantly who you are and what you do. Having a fan page helps with SEO and allows for extra visibility and traffic from search engines. The following are the six types of fan pages you can choose from on Facebook:

1. Local business or place
2. Brand or product
3. Artist, band or Public figure
4. Entertainment
5. Cause or Community

Step 2: Add a Logo and other images to your fan page.

Upload a photo of yourself, your logo (if you have one), and an image of your book cover. Your photos should give visitors an instant understanding of your business and the books, products, and services you provide.

Step 3: Fill in the details. Let everyone know what your page is about.

Fill in the basic information about yourself and your business and add your website URL. What you write here helps create first impressions. Use the right personality and voice to represent your business well.

How to be More Social on Facebook

If you plan to promote your book on Facebook, you need to be active on social media. You need to join groups, like fan pages, and interact with people you friended on Facebook. Here are a few tips that you can use to be more social on Facebook.

1. Look for funny videos, photos, stories or blog posts and share them on Facebook.
2. Post a funny photo or video as a status update on your personal profile.
3. Like and comment on any new activity in your newsfeed.
4. Post information related to your book on your fan page and in your groups.
5. Like and comment on any new activity in your groups and on your pages.
6. Post articles from your blog to your main newsfeed and ask for "likes" and "shares".
7. Also post articles from your blog to all relevant fan pages and groups.
8. Thank people for reading and ask them to leave a comment in the box below your articles.

What to Post on Facebook

So now that you have created your Facebook fan page you need to start posting messages that are relevant to your book and your niche which your fans will find interesting. Many authors have difficulty trying to figure out what to post on their pages and what message they want to share with their fans. Here are a few ideas of what you can post on your fan page to attract your fans and to encourage them to buy your book.

1. Inspirational quotes. There are thousands of inspirational and motivational quotes online. Do a Google search for 'motivational quotes' and you can share these on your fan page.

2. Share niche related blog posts and articles. Set up Google Alerts for any keywords related to your niche and get attention-grabbing stories sent to your inbox that you can share with your fans.

3. Share photos, videos, and articles that other people have posted on their pages and newsfeed.

4. Post fun videos and pictures that are somewhat related to your niche.

5. Share your own blog posts

6. Post updates of the book you are currently writing and free book promotions.

7. Share any special events that are related to your niche.

How to Use Facebook Advertising to Promote Your Book

Creating and maintaining a fan page is not the only way to promote your book. Facebook also offers an advertising service to help you to reach more people with your message. Paid advertising can be an effective way to spread the word about your new book. You can also advertise your website and your fan page to get more likes. With Facebook advertising you get to choose how much money you want to spend to promote your book and you can target the people you want to reach. Keep the following factors in mind when you set up your advertising campaign.

Identify your target market.

The great thing about Facebook advertising is that you can be specific in the kind of people you want to reach. Choosing your demographic will determine the number of people who will see your ad and how much it will cost you. Choose the country, city, gender, age range, likes and dislikes. The more specific you are, the better your chances of having an impact on the people who see your ad.

Create an attention-grabbing headline

You need to create a headline that draws people's attention. If you wrote a book that is similar to *The Four-Hour Work Week* written by Timothy Ferriss you can target readers who have a preference for his books. For example, your headline could read: "Want to Earn More and Work Less?" It is very important to target the market based on their interests or else you will be wasting money on clicks and you will get poor results. So make sure that you have a powerful, targeted headline that attracts your target audience.

Use an Eye-Catching Image and Text.

Facebook only allows you to enter a few lines of text in the body of the ad so you need to make it count. You want to make sure that people click on your ad so you need to write compelling text or include a call to action, for example, 'Download now' or 'Buy now'. Your image also needs to be compelling so that it attracts your target audience to your ad. If you are going to use your book cover, make sure that it looks good as a thumbnail size image. The picture and the title of the book should be clear for people to read. You can link your ad to your Amazon sales page or to your website where people can buy your book.

Determine Your Budget and the Length of Your Advertising Campaign.

Facebook gives you full control of how much you can spend and how long you want to run your ad campaign. The minimum daily budget for an ad campaign could start as low as $2.00 per day. Make sure you set an end date for your campaign or else you will keep spending money.

Boost Posts on Your Facebook Fan Page

Another effective marketing tool you can use to increase the number of views to your fan page is to boost your posts. Simply follow the steps below to boost posts on your page.

1. Go to your fan page and click on Boost Post in the lower right corner of a post you created.
2. Choose your target audience and set a budget based on the number of people you want to reach and the length of time you want your boost to run.
3. Click Boost Post.

Chapter 11: How to Use YouTube to Promote Your Book

A great way to gain wider exposure of your book and to boost sales is to promote your book on YouTube. You can create a video and upload it to YouTube for free. This video sharing website has millions of visits every day and this can be a very powerful marketing tool that can be very beneficial to self-published authors.

Google is the owner of YouTube, therefore YouTube is the second largest search engine on the internet. This gives you as a self-published author the opportunity to submit informative videos and place them in front of people who will most likely purchase your book.

In order to promote your book on YouTube, you need to set up a YouTube channel. This can be easily done in minutes and you can immediately upload your first video. The following are steps you can take to promote your book effectively on YouTube.

Step 1: If you have a Google email address then you can use this to open an account on YouTube. After you set up your account, you need to come up with a name for your channel. Because you are promoting your book I recommend that you use your own name for your channel. This helps your readers to find you on YouTube and to become fans of your book.

Step 2: Next, create your channel artwork and logo. The channel artwork is the header that people will see when they visit your channel. You can use your book cover to create the header and your photo as the logo. You will need to upload your book cover and photo through your Google + account. YouTube provides a guide to show you how to do this at https://support.google.com/youtube/answer/1646861?hl=en-GB.

Step 3: Once you have set up your channel you should also create a YouTube channel trailer. The trailer plays automatically when people visit your page. The length of your trailer should be approximately 1 minute long and should give your visitors an idea of what your channel is about and encourage them to subscribe.

Step 4: After you create your channel trailer you can then create and upload your first video. You can use a smartphone, a digital camera or screen capture recording software such as Camtasia or

Camstudio. First create presentation slides in PowerPoint and then record them with the screen capture recording software.

Once you have published your nonfiction book, you can use the book's content to create informative videos for your viewers. There are five ways you can use your book content to create useful videos:

1. Create a book trailer that explains what your book is about, what the chapters are, and how it will be of benefit to the reader.
2. Create a video of each chapter of your book.
3. Don't forget to promote your book at the end of your video. Include the book cover, where your book can be purchased, and a call to action to buy the book. You can also add a link to your book's sales page or to your website in the video description. In the video you should also ask your viewers to buy your book and leave a review on Amazon once they have read it.
4. Additionally, you can use your video to encourage your viewers to follow you on Twitter or connect with you on Facebook.

There are so many ways that you can use YouTube to promote your book. One of the ways is to create a book trailer. Whether you are a new or established author, you should take advantage of this popular video sharing site to spread the word about your book.

How to Create a Book Trailer

Book trailers are a great marketing tool for promoting your books. You don't need any expensive software and you don't need to be a professional camera person. You don't even need an expensive camera. The only tools you need are free and they are already available on your computer.

The items you need to make a good book trailer are software such as Microsoft Office PowerPoint, Windows Live Movie Maker, and a lot of pictures that you either took yourself with your camera or images you downloaded from photo websites.

Additionally you also need a little imagination. You wrote your book, you know it well, and only you can come up with a proper book trailer that tells viewers exactly what your book is about. So let's get started!

Step 1: Write a Script

It helps to write your thoughts down on paper. Sometimes an idea may pop into your head when you least expect it. Sometimes it can happen in the most awkward situations, and you need to grab a pen and paper to write it down before you forget.

This is when inspiration strikes and you have got to write it down. It doesn't have to be perfect. Your script could start with the title of your book and the picture. You can list the table of contents and a brief description of what each section is about. If you wrote a novel then you can come up with a compelling description of the plot.

Step 2: Search for Pictures

You may have photos that you took yourself or pictures saved on your computer that you planned to use in the future. If you have neither of these then you can search for pictures online.

A word of caution, though, you have to be careful where you download your pictures from because some of them may be copyrighted and you cannot use the picture without the owner's permission. Do a Google search and enter the keywords "free royalty free images". In the search results you should find a list of websites where you can get royalty free images that you can use in your video. Just make sure that you read the terms and conditions for using the images. Two great sites where you can find royalty free pictures for your book trailer is FreeDigitalPhotos.net and Pixabay.

You can also purchase photos from photo sites like Dreamstime and iStockphoto. Create a folder on your computer where you can store all the pictures for your book trailer so that you can find them easily.

Step 3: Design Your Book Trailer in PowerPoint

1. Open up PowerPoint and first choose a design. You could put the title of your book or a picture on the first slide. You should also include a link to your website (if you have one) at the bottom. You can change the font, font size, colour, insert pictures, etc.

2. When you have completed your first slide click on the **Home** tab at the top and click **New Slide**.

3. On slide 2 you can add whatever you want such as another picture, a graph, or just text. Do the same for the next slide.

You can do whatever you want to each slide. Keep adding new slides and filling them in until you have completed the whole slide presentation.

4. Click **File**, **Save As**, and choose the folder where you want to save your PowerPoint slides.

5. Then choose to **Save the File as** a Jpeg. Select to save all slides in your presentation as Jpeg files. A new folder will be created where all of your slides have been saved as Jpeg. Now it is time to put all these slides together to make a video.

Step 4: Open up Windows Live Movie Maker.

1. Click **Add Videos and Photos**. Find the folder where your slides were saved and select the first slide. Continue to do this until you have added all the slides to make your video.

2. Then click **Add Music**. If your video does not require any music then you can skip this step. If it does need music then select the folder that holds your music and click **Open**. Make sure that you select music that you are permitted to use.

3. Include a **Title** and **Credits** if you choose.

4. Next choose an **Auto Movie Theme** to be included in your project.

5. You can preview the whole video by clicking the **View** tab and previewing the whole video in full screen. When you are satisfied with the way your video plays then you can publish it to your computer. If you do not select a folder, the video will automatically be saved in your Videos folder.

Step 5: Create an Account at YouTube.com

Now that you have created your book trailer video, it is time to upload it to YouTube. If you already have a Gmail account you can simply sign in and click the Upload button to upload your video.

If you don't have a Gmail account then you can sign up for one by visiting Google.com and clicking on Gmail at the top. In YouTube follow the instructions to set up your account. Set up your profile by adding a photo or a logo if you have one.

Write a short description of what your video is about. Be sure to include a link to your website at the top of the description. Also include keywords so that people will be able to find your video.

Step 6: Upload Your Video to Other Video Sites

You can repeat step 5 for other video sites. Simply sign up for an account, edit your profile, and upload your video. There are many other video sites where you can submit your book trailer video to. Some of the most popular sites are Daily Motion, Veoh, and Vimeo.

Chapter 12: Send Out Press Releases

As part of your marketing campaign you should include press releases. As an author, writing a press release gives you the opportunity to connect to your target audience as well as to reporters. Don't be afraid to leave your contact details so that reporters can contact you for an interview as well as request a copy of your book. Here are a few tips to help you write a compelling press release.

1. **Write an attention-grabbing headline.** A successful press release starts with an irresistible headline. Make your title short and simple. It should only be one line. Use action verbs and make your title clear and easy to understand. Your headline should be so interesting that it entices people to read the rest of the press release. For example, a compelling headline could read: "C.E. John Explores Web Designing with WordPress in her New Book".

2. **Be clear about why you are writing the press release.** In the first paragraph your release should cover who, what, where, when, why and how of the launch of your new book. You should not include any new information after this section because the reader might miss it.

3. **Include a quote from yourself the author, or from an expert whom you may have interviewed for your book.** Adding a quote to your press release brings it to life and it gives people an idea of how your news will impact your readers.

4. **Provide Valuable Background Information.** Include in your press release some information about what inspired you to write your book.

5. **Explain clearly what your press release is actually about what you do as an author.** Explain the type of books that you write about and include a link to your blog or website.

Always keep in mind that the reason you are writing a press release is to get media attention for your book so that they may review it and discuss it, which will potentially boost your book sales. There are other key items that you should also consider when writing your press release.

You can also use a press release as an opportunity to send out copies of your book to get reviewed and to get interviews about your book. Always include in your press release a line that says: "Review Copies and Interviews Upon Request". If you get a good book review in a magazine or get an interview on TV or radio, this will help you to sell more books.

If you need book reviews, send your press release to professionals who write book reviews and interview authors. It is best to send your press release by email.

Try to write multiple press releases from different angles and send them out to targeted professional reviewers. This will help to build repeated exposure of your book and to get online media outlets and bloggers to notice your book.

The following is an example of how a press release should be formatted. You can use this example as a template to write your own press release.

Company Name

Address 1, Address 2, City, State, Postcode

Website

Tel: 0000-000-0000

Fax: 0000-000-0000

Email: info@website.com

PRESS RELEASE

FOR IMMEDIATE RELEASE

Contact: Name of Contact

Tel: 0000-000-0000

Mob: 0000-000-000

[Headline/Title]

First Paragraph: Details as to what the press release is about, such as who, what, where, when, why and how?

Second Paragraph: Who cares? Why should you care? Where can one find it? When will it happen? [Include quote]

Third Paragraph: Summarize the press release. Give further information about the author or the company. Include contact information.

###

The following are examples of press releases that authors and publishers have used to promote books:

Simon and Schuster

(http://www.simonandschuster.biz:80/press_releases)

Hachette Book Group

(http://www.hachettebookgroup.com/media-and-publicity/press-releases)

Once you have completed and are satisfied with your press release, you can submit it to the following websites:

www.webwire.com

www.globenewswire.com

www.businesswire.com

www.prweb.com

www.free-press-release.com

www.prnewswire.com

www.prlog.com

www.24-7pressrelease.com

Chapter 13: How to Use Slideshows to Promote Your Book

Another effective marketing tool to help increase exposure of your book is to create slideshows and upload them to Slideshare. Unfortunately, Slideshare is a social media site which is often overlooked by many authors, but it has great potential for the purposes of book marketing. There are three key steps that you should follow to ensure that you promote your book successfully.

Step 1: Create a Compelling Presentation Using PowerPoint

1. Open Microsoft PowerPoint on your computer.
2. Click the **Design** tab at the top of the screen. The tool bar will change to different design options. Choose a design you like or you can create your own design from scratch.
3. Change the colour, font and effects of the design by clicking on the relevant button on the tool bar.
4. Enter your information on the first slide. You can put the title of your book or a picture of your book cover on the first slide. You can also add the URL to your website at the bottom of every slide. Change the font, font size, insert pictures, etc. if it is necessary.

5. When you have completed your first slide, you can either go to the slide menu on the left side of the screen, right click and select duplicate slide, or click on the **Home** tab, click **New Slide**, and select a slide theme that you would like to use next.

6. On slide 2, remove the text and pictures you don't want to use and then add some new information and images to this slide.

7. Continue to add more slides and include whatever you want in each slide. Just make sure that you do not reveal too much information from your book. You should have at least 10 to 15 slides in total.

8. Try to include eye-catching images to your slideshow. Adding images to your presentation will make it look more appealing and people will more likely share your presentation with others.

Step 2: Include a Call to Action to Buy Your Book

Your objective to creating a slideshow presentation is to increase sales of your book. Therefore, you need to include two slides in your presentation which focus on promoting your book. You can place the first promotional slide somewhere in the middle of your presentation and put the second one at the end. For example, if your presentation consists of 30 slides, you would insert your book promotion info on slide 15. Once you have completed your presentation you can save it and then upload it to Slideshare.

Step 3: Share Your Presentation

Slideshare gives you plenty of options to share your presentation. You can embed your presentation on your website or blog and you can post a link to it on social media. Slideshare makes it so easy to share your presentation by providing social media buttons at the bottom. You can post a link to your presentation on Facebook, Twitter, LinkedIn, and Pinterest. You can also send it by email. Here are two excellent examples of book promotion slideshow presentations:

8 Strategies to Feel Energized Every Single Morning by Steve Scott
http://bit.ly/1LmoS9K

Career Change by Joanna Penn
http://bit.ly/1LZSY5E

Chapter 14: Submit Your Book to Top Book Listing Sites

Your book promotion campaign would be incomplete if you did not include book listing sites as part of your marketing plan. When you submit your book to other book listing sites you make your book available to a wider audience. The great thing about these sites is that they have their own subscriber list in which they email a list of books daily or weekly. I have used many of these sites to promote my books and they have been very effective in increasing my book sales. The following are online book listing sites where you can submit your book for free. Some of the sites offer extra services for a small fee.

Awesome Gang

Awesome Gang provides a submission form that is easy to fill out and is free. This site allows you to include a synopsis (description) of your book. You can include your author bio. Add your website, Facebook Fan Page, and a link to your book on Amazon. Upload a cover image of your book. To gain more exposure, you have the option to pay $10 to get your book listed on the front page for 2 days, a guaranteed spot in their newsletters, and your book will also be included on their social media channels.

http://awesomegang.com/submit-your-book/

BookGoodies.com

Book Goodies offers free book submission of your free book promos for Kindle and Smashwords. You must register as a member first in order to submit your book. Posts of your free book promotion on the same day only goes to the BookGoodies Forum. This site also offers other book submission opportunities but you must pay for these services. Prices range from $5 to $40. The form is easy to fill out. You can pay for your book submission through PayPal.

http://bookgoodies.com/authors-start-here/

FreeBookDude.com

Use this site to list your free Amazon Kindle Book. The form is very easy to fill out and you can list your book for free when you have a free Kindle book promotion. This site also offers other paid promotion packages such as Featured Book Promotion Packages and Sidebar Ads at various prices. You can also write a guest post on this website.

http://www.freebookdude.com/2014/03/list-your-free-amazon-kindle-books.html

AuthorMarketingClub.com

This is one of the best sites on the web for free book submissions. Author Marketing Club accepts books from all different types of genres. You need to register to become a member before you can submit your book. Submission is free and the form is very easy to fill out.

Only submit your book when you have free book promotion days on Amazon. Your book will be sent by email to thousands of readers. They send you an email to confirm the submission of your book. Be sure to submit your book a couple of days before the actual date of your free book promotion day on Amazon.

http://www.authormarketingclub.com/

FreeDiscountedBooks.com

Your e-book must be temporarily free through Amazon KDP and you will need to create an account at this site. They send confirmation by email that your book has been submitted. You may have to pay $5 to guarantee that your book is listed on this website.

http://freediscountedbooks.com/submit/

BookHitch.com

This is a search engine for books. You must register to sign up for an account and to be able to list your books. It is free to list your books on this site but you can also upgrade to a premium service for $19.95. The form is easy to fill out and your book will be listed, viewed and searchable immediately.

http://www.bookhitch.com/addbook.aspx

Published.com

This is a free book directory that promotes the best books. You can join this website for free and the form is very easy to fill out. You must provide the ISBN number of your book and links to Amazon, Barnes and Noble, your website and anywhere else your book can be purchased online.

https://www.published.com/join1.aspx

Pretty-Hot.com

You can submit your book for free to this site. They also offer a featured option for $25 that guarantees a featured spot on the home page for 5 days. Your book will also be promoted through their newsletter and on Twitter and Facebook. The form is easy to fill out and you can add a link to your Facebook page and Twitter profile page.

http://pretty-hot.com/submit-your-book/

Nothing Binding

Nothing Binding is a website that was created for independent authors as well as unpublished writers. This website gives authors the opportunity to showcase their work to readers. Nothing Binding offers free membership and book promotion opportunities at its sister website WritersReaders.com. It is very easy to join Nothing Binding. Simply enter a username and password to create your account.

http://www.nothingbinding.com/

Book Daily

You can set up a free author account and get immediate exposure for your book at BookDaily.com. When you join BookDaily.com, you will have the opportunity to post the first chapter of your book for readers to view, post your author bio and photo, include a link to your website or blog, upload a video about your book, and receive a regular author marketing newsletter. The only limitation to the website is that you can only add five of your own books to

BookDaily.com. If you want to add more you will have to send a request to them by email.

http://www.bookdaily.com/

Indie Book of the Day (IBD)

If you want to boost more downloads of your book then you should join IndieBookoftheDay.com. If you have planned free book promotion days for your Kindle book then IBD can help you to reach more readers and get more free downloads of your book. As an author you will have the opportunity to promote your book on the IBD website, Facebook page, Twitter and Pinterest. The form is easy to fill out and can be completed in less than 10 minutes.

http://indiebookoftheday.com/authors/free-on-kindle-listing/

Quick Action Plan

If you are going to promote and sell your books, then you need to have a plan. This book shows you 14 simple ways to promote your book which have worked for me and I hope will work for you. To help you get started, I have included this quick action plan so that you can easily follow each step to promote your book online.

1. Create a sales page. Identify your target audience and arouse their attention, interest, desire, and action.

2. Set up an author page on Amazon's Author Central website. Include a photo and author bio.

3. Optimize your book for Amazon. Use your best keywords, create a personal profile, choose the right category, and use the Look Inside Feature for your book.

4. Get book reviews.

5. Schedule a free book promotion through Kindle Direct Publishing.

6. Create an author website. Register a domain name, set up web hosting, and build your site with WordPress.

7. Submit your website to the top three search engines: Google, Yahoo and Bing.

8. Build an email list. Sign up with an email service provider, create an opt-in form, add code to your website, and get subscribers.

9. Create a Twitter profile and use this instant messaging service to promote your book. Get followers, use hashtags, interact with people, and ask for book reviews.

10. Start a Facebook fan page. Advertise and boost posts on Facebook.

11. Open an account at YouTube. Create a book trailer video and upload it to YouTube and other video sharing websites.

12. Send out press releases.

13. Create a slideshow presentation and upload to Slideshare. Share your presentation on social media.

14. Submit your book to the top book listing sites.

Conclusion

Promoting your book shouldn't have to be difficult and it shouldn't force you to empty your bank account. Creating a sales page, setting up your author profile, designing a website to showcase your books, and using social media to gain exposure of your book are just some of the ways that you can successfully promote your book. By simply applying all of the methods described in this book you will see a significant increase in sales and your book marketing campaign will be a success.

Thank You

I hope that you found this guide to writing your nonfiction book to be very helpful. I want to say thank you for purchasing this book and for reading it all the way to the end.

I would be honoured if you could please leave a review for this book *How to Make Money Promoting and Selling a Nonfiction Book* on Amazon.

If you feel that this book answered your questions as to how to publish a nonfiction book, then please do not hesitate to share it with your friends, family members and colleagues.

If you have any further questions or comments about this book or on writing in general, please contact me at the following email address:

ChristineJohnBooks@gmail.com

About the Author

"Writing books that inspire and help people to succeed."

Whether you need information about designing a website, writing a book, or finding a job, Christine provides the books that satisfy your needs.

Christine has written books on a variety of topics that help and inspire authors, bloggers, internet marketers, entrepreneurs, and job seekers. Included in the mix are books written for the entertainment and enjoyment of people who love to read romance novels, short stories and poetry. She has also written information to motivate individuals to reach their true potential and to succeed in life.

Christine enjoys inspiring and motivating people to develop themselves both personally and professionally, and to be more creative.

When she is not busy working on her next book, Christine enjoys reading, travelling, and helping young entrepreneurs to make their dreams a reality. Presently, Christine lives in the United Kingdom where she continues to share her knowledge with the world.

If you want to find out more, check out the books that Christine has published on Amazon.com or Amazon.co.uk. Also visit her website for more information at ChristineJohnBooks.com.

Connect with Christine

Facebook
https://www.facebook.com/ChristineJohnBooks

Twitter
https://twitter.com/CejohnBooks

LinkedIn
https://uk.linkedin.com/in/cejohn

Google Plus
www.google.com/+Christinejohnbooks77

YouTube
https://www.youtube.com/user/SpringMediaIntl

More Books by Christine John

Visit your local Amazon website to download the following books to your computer or Kindle. These books are also available in Print format. Go to Amazon to place your order now!

Nonfiction

How to Write a Nonfiction Book that Sells

How to Publish a Nonfiction Book for Free Using Kindle Direct Publishing, CreateSpace and Smashwords

WordPress for Beginners: The Easy Step by Step Guide to Creating a Website with WordPress

How to Start and Run an Online Business

How to Get the Job You Want

Fiction

Last Chance

The Runaway Bride

Short Stories for Teenagers

Poetry

Poems About Life